PROJECT MANAGEMENT

Introduction to Project Management for Business Students

Mario Chinas

Chinas, Mario.
PROJECT MANAGEMENT: Introduction to Project Management for Business Students - 2nd ed.
Includes bibliographical references.
ISBN: 978-9925-7383-4-2

Webpage: https://www.mccebooks.com

TABLE OF CONTENTS

PREFACE

Welcome to the 2nd edition of *PROJECT MANAGEMENT: Introduction to Project Management for Business Students.*

This book aims to introduce the concept of Project Management by providing the fundamental theory of the topic in question in a clear and concise manner. The field of Project Management is huge so we focus our discussion on some of the most popular areas: Human Resources and Time & Budget Management.

Our series of Books for Business Students are concise and targeted to maximizing your 'value for time', i.e. to give you the maximum essential learning on the subject matter in the shortest time.

As you will notice, our Books are written in a style and format that emulates essay writing. The aim is to familiarise you, the reader, with the format and style expected in essay writing, providing a bridge between the study material and the output you will be expected to deliver in your essay projects and essay based exams. Moreover they provide a wealth of references / bibliography, saving you valuable time that you can utilise to further enhance your work.

INTRODUCTION

Managing projects is one of the most challenging endeavours a manager can face. Each project is at least somewhat unique in the process it uses or in the desired outcome. Firstly let us define project; a project is 'a temporary endeavor undertaken to produce a unique product, service, or result" (PMBOK, 2004, p. 5). Projects are by definition finite, low-volume, high-variety activities. A project should have definite starting and ending points, a budget, a clearly defined scope of work to be done, and specific performance requirements that must be met (Lewis, 2007).

Project management is defined as the 'application of knowledge, skills, tools and techniques to project activities to achieve project requirements' (PMBOK, 2004, p. 8). The project manager has the responsibility to ensure that the project is completed on time, within the set budget, and meets the set objectives for the project. In order to accomplish this the project manager must manage the resources available for the project (including human resources), plan the work and work schedule in collaboration with those who will perform the tasks, facilitate communication so that everyone has the necessary information to ensure smooth operations, etc (Lewis, 2007).

A project begins with the definition of its purpose. If the project is not correctly defined, it will most probably fail as the result will not meet stakeholder's expectations. The stakeholders in any project are the individuals and groups who have an interest in the project outcome. Various stakeholders are likely to have different views on a project's objectives that may conflict with other stakeholders. Therefore involving stakeholders in the process of project definition is useful in preventing objections and problems later in the project. Project managers should solicit the opinions of powerful stakeholders when shaping the project objectives as this will make it more likely that they will support the project at later stages (Slack et al, 2007).

Moreover communicating with stakeholders early and frequently can ensure that they fully understand the project and understand potential benefits. More importantly, the feedback will indicate what actions are needed to prevent opposition or build support (Slack et al, 2007).

PROJECT DEFINITION

A project can only be completed if the end result is clearly defined; thus the first thing that must be done is to clarify the project definition. A project is defined by its desired end result (i.e. its objectives), its scope (the work content), and the way in which the project will be carried out and monitored (Rowbotham et al, 2007).

Stakeholders are often informed of a project's objectives and scope by use of a formal document called a 'statement of work'. This is short statement that sums up the essence of the project, documenting the project's objectives and scope (Brennan, 2011). It is often presented as a clear and concise one page statement that sums up the essence of the project. It can be a useful tool to promote understanding and a vision for the project's team members and other project stakeholders. As changes to project scope are often the cause of project failure, it is imperative that the statement clearly defines the boundaries of the project (Lewis, 2007).

KEY ROLES

Often a project champion is assigned to support the project manager. A project champion is a person, usually in senior management, who supports and promotes the project. The project champion assists the project manager by ensuring the cooperation of stakeholders and facilitating the manager's work (Stevenson, 2002).

PROJECT MANAGEMENT -
PLANNING & CONTROL

Managing a project is a challenging task that faces many uncertainties; thus it is not possible to ensure with certainty that a project will be completed within a set deadline, as many unforeseen circumstances may arise. However, proper planning for all foreseeable events and monitoring & controlling of progress will maximise the chances of completing the project within the set deadline.

Proper planning requires the adherence to a formal process. The traditional process for project management is separated into five stages / phases: initiating, planning, executing, monitoring and controlling, and closing (Kamauff, 2010). In the literature the number of stages may differ, but the underlying logic is the same across all variations of the process.

As mentioned, proper planning and control will maximise the chances of completing the project within the set deadline. We will thus focus on these two elements of project management; however these cannot take place without first initiating the project.

In initiating the project, the objective of the project and its scope must be determined, as well as an assessment of its feasibility and a cost benefit analysis that justifies proceeding with the project. Once again, of particular importance is the desired output which must be clearly defined and agreed with all stakeholders from the start. If the project is not clearly defined from the beginning, the schedule and the budget cannot be correctly set and thus the project will not succeed. As we have seen previously, one method of documenting the project's objectives and scope is a 'statement of work' (Brennan, 2011).

The planning phase is particularly challenging for a project manager. Moreover, when the deadline is tight, or when the project is overly complex, that is when planning becomes really important and requires even more detail (Lewis, 2007). The plan must start with the basics, i.e. the project objectives, and go into full detail on all activities that need to be completed. It must answer questions such as what must be done, by whom, for how much, how, when, and so on (Lewis, 2007).

The scope, which was already determined in the initial phase, must be fully clarified, especially what the project does not cover, in order to avoid misunderstandings and to assist in the correct planning of activities (Kamauff, 2010). Moreover any constraints must be considered and documented.

Once the scope details have been established, a list of all the activities necessary must be composed. Depending on the complexity of the project, the input of team members or other experts may be necessary. Especially if the team members are inexperienced in the subject matter, new employees or "entry-level" consulting staff, the advice of other experts may be required to ensure that no activities are neglected or miscalculated.

At this point we must start formulating our budgets, time/cost estimates, cash flow charts, logistics (material availability planning), etc. According to Lewis (2007) to plan a project properly, you must attend to three kinds of activities that may have to be performed during the lifecycle of the project. These are strategy, tactics, and logistics. Strategy refers to the overall method you will employ to do the work. Tactics is where you answer the who, what, when, how and where questions. Logistics attends to ensuring that the resources necessary are available when needed.

However, we first also must put the identified activities in some logical order. This is normally done using a Work Breakdown Structure (WBS); a hierarchical listing of what needs to be done during the project (Stevenson, 2002). The first step in constructing a WBS is to identify the major elements in the project and to break them down to their supporting activities, sub-activities, etc, until you cover all activities that need to be performed to complete the project. The usefulness of a WBS is that it allows the project manager to determine exactly what needs to be done, identify the relationships and estimate time and cost for each part of the project.

Having identified all activities and put them in a logical order we can proceed to create a schedule for the project. Scheduling involves the detailed allocation of resources to activities (Bamford

& Forrester, 2010). It is not a one off process, since it needs to be monitored and updated as the project execution progresses. To assist with project scheduling we will need to make use of project management tools (such as Gantt charts) and network analysis tools (such as the Critical Path Method and Programme Evaluation and Review Technique).

The Gantt chart is a graphical representation of the production plan which exhibits in a simple way the overall project plan. They are simple to read and thus considered an excellent tool to use for communicating to team members what they need to do within given time frames. However because of its simplistic nature, the Gantt chart does not assist the project manager in optimizing the project plan, since the chart does not provide the necessary detail of information needed to reveal how a delay in one activity will affect other activities and thus does not reveal critical activities (Brown et al, 2001). For this network analysis tools are used.

The two most frequently used network analysis tools are the Programme Evaluation and Review Technique (PERT) and the Critical Path Method (CPM). Both of these provide a graphical display (network diagram) of the project's activities that enables project managers to estimate the duration of the project, the critical activities for timely completion of the project and an indication of how long any activity can be delayed without delaying the project (Stevenson, 2002). Although PERT and CPM are not identical, from a conceptual standpoint their differences are minor. CPM is more suited to projects were the design concepts are known, since it only uses one estimate of task duration for each activity into account. PERT is mostly used in projects that have a large amount of uncertainty in design and construction as it allows for situations where timings cannot be estimated with certainty; it utilises three estimates of duration for each activity, the optimistic, the most likely and the pessimistic (Roy, 2005). The scope of this paper does not allow us to go into further detail, but the important point is to be aware of the choice between CPM and PERT.

In constructing the network diagram there are two basic types; 'activity on arrow' and 'activity on node'. Activity on arrow is where the activity is represented by an arrow and the nodes at the beginning and the end of the arrow are events; for example a node at project start, an arrow for the first activity leading to a node of completion of the first activity. Activity on node is where an activity is represented by a node and the arrows between the nodes simply indicate dependency. Of the two methods, activity on arrow is the most used in project networks (Bramford & Forrester, 2010). A simple example is given below.

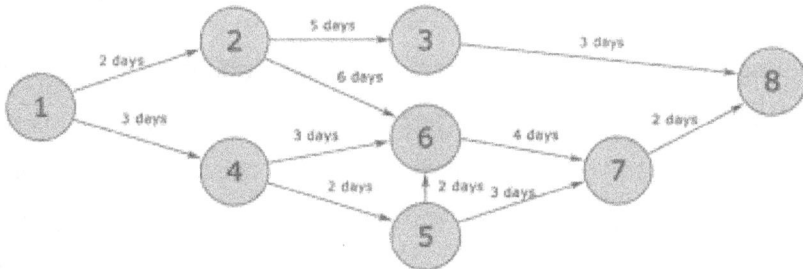

Once the network diagram has been prepared the critical path through the network can be identified; this is the chain of tasks that represents the longest 'distance' (i.e. duration) through the project. Any delay of an activity on the critical path will result in a delay of the project completion date (Kamauff, 2010). As most projects must be completed against set time deadlines, the critical path is of increased importance. In the above example the critical path is 1-2-6-7-8, with 14 days.

We must also keep in mind that the project environment must be considered. According to Rowbotham et al (2007) Planning and Controlling depends on a clear understanding of the project environment and the project definition. The environment influences the way a project is carried out, and the nature of the environment in which a project takes place is the main determinant of the uncertainty surrounding it (Slack et al, 2007). The project environment refers to the factors that may influence the product during its life cycle. This covers a wide array of factors, from supply of raw materials to political instability. It is in essence a PEST (or PESTLE) analysis of the environment in which the project will be developed – Political, Economic, Social, Technological, Legal and Environmental (natural environment) issues that could have a direct or indirect effect on the project. Although these issues are generally beyond the control of the project manager contingency plans should exist for those factors that can be anticipated; for example how a storm or other bad weather might affect work progress and what can be done to minimise any delays.

Another planning concept which may be of particular use

considering the time constraints of our project is the Critical Chain Project Planning (Brown et al, 2001). The aim of this concept is to overcome some of the main reasons that projects fail to be completed on time. Put simply this concept stipulates that activities are started as soon as the previous activities have finished, which in theory will usually be sooner than estimated because activity durations are estimates that normally include some slack for normal delays. With predefined starting times the time saved from activities that finish early is wasted instead of being used to offset late finishes of other activities. However, putting this concept into practice depends on the ability of the next activity being able to start early; it may require resources that will not be available earlier even if the preceding activity (or activities) is completed.

Having completed our planning, we can proceed to the execution of the project. During execution monitoring and control must take place continually to ensure that everything is running as planned and that we are on schedule. Monitoring & Control involve such activities as monitoring work progress, activity completion times, costs, resource usage, and performance. Where necessary the project manager must intervene and make any changes required to bring the actual performance in line with the original plan. (Rowbotham et al, 2007). For control to be effective, a formal control process should be established. This will need to address issues such as what will be monitored, by whom, where will monitoring results be recorded and how frequently. Feedback and reporting is very important at this stage in order to keep on top of everything that is happening (Brennan, 2011). Control sheets / activity update sheets can be used for reporting at regular intervals; the use of project management software could greatly assist especially in large complex projects. In most cases the most unpredictable aspect to monitor is time; whether the active tasks are proceeding as planned. However we should keep in mind that time, cost, and quality are interrelated. An activity may be ahead of time either because of additional resources (eg manpower) thus increasing cost or due to hasty, poorer quality work. Via monitoring and control we must ensure not only that activities are on time, but within budget and of the quality stipulated in the scope.

COMMON ISSUES

Commonly projects exceed budget and fall behind schedule. This may occur for a variety of reasons such as changes to user requirements (known as user change orders) and increasing conflicts in the requirements of various different users.

The occurrence of frequent user change orders and increasing conflicts in user requirements indicates that possibly the end users were not involved in the process of the project definition, or that they do not realise the scope of the project and thus have unrealistic demands and expectations.

Discussions with the main stakeholders should clarify if the original objectives and scope need to be amended. This could be done by setting a meeting with all the relevant stakeholders with an agenda to reaffirm the project objectives and scope. The end result must be the agreement of specific objectives & scope and the commitment of all stakeholders to what has been agreed.

It is important to understand that if a change in scope is necessary, then the project manager should accept and embrace this, not resist it - the project managers job is not to stop scope change, but to successfully manage that change. No matter how carefully a project has been planned, changes may need to be made throughout its life cycle. This is one of the most important areas of a project, as the cost of implementing changes can be significant. Therefore, it is best to minimise the occurrence of changes by following the planning process thoroughly from the start, and deal with any changes in an organised and controlled way.

Scope change control procedures should be specified, which will clarify how changes will be managed over the life of the project and by whom they will be approved (Lewis, 2007). Scope change control is the process of reviewing all change requests, approving and managing changes, and reflecting these in the deliverables, project documents and project plan.

The project planning phase involved the definition of work specification, determination of quantity of work, and estimation of resources required. Based on the review of the objectives & scope the whole planning process will need to be reviewed and updated in order to incorporate the new parameters. In effect the process of project planning will need to be repeated (Rowbotham et al, 2007), as if starting a new project from the beginning, building on the knowledge of the existing plan to formulate a new plan that will allow for successful project completion. Likewise, the monitoring & control procedures may need to be reviewed.

The activity list will need to be reviewed and updated, as well as the network diagram, in order to identify the critical path for project completion. If a network diagram was not previously utilized and the critical path not identified, these should be implemented now as they are invaluable tools for project management. The critical path method provides not only an excellent way of calculating the shortest completion time and the critical activities for a project, but also a framework to analyze the time/cost trade-off (Babu & Suresh, 1996 and Khang & Myint, 1999).

TIME, COST, SCOPE TRADE-OFF

In agreeing / reaffirming the scope, the time and cost of the project should be taken into consideration. A project duration can be shortened by increasing personnel or equipment, or / and by reducing the scope. Similarly cost may be reduced by extending the duration and reducing personnel or equipment, or / and by reducing the scope.

Obviously at first the project manager will attempt to adjust the schedule and the expenses so as to stay within the budgeted time and cost. However it may not be possible to achieve the desired scope within the initial budgeted time and cost.

If both time and cost cannot exceed the original budget, then the scope must be decreased for the project to produce a meaningful result by the completion date. If the scope cannot be reduced and completing the project within the deadline is imperative, then some allowance for increased cost will have to be made.

We will refer to the process of reorganizing project systems and resources to get the project back on track as Project Realignment.

PROJECT REALIGNMENT

Once the project definition has been reaffirmed, we will need to take corrective action. As the project has fallen behind schedule we will need to examine if we can speed up the remaining activities in order to finish the project by the deadline. One method to achieve this without increasing costs is by the Tradeoff of Resources (Roy, 2005). Another proposed method is through the use of Work Study techniques (Roy, 2005). A further method which we can utilize to shorten the duration of a project in the cheapest manner possible is called 'Crashing Networks' (or 'Project Crashing' or simply 'Crashing') (Heizer & Render, 2004). Lastly we will examine an alternative planning concept which aims to overcome some of the main reasons that projects fail to be completed on time: Critical Chain Project Planning (Brown et al, 2001).

Tradeoff of resources

The most cost effective method to reduce project duration is the tradeoff or transfer of resources. This method involves the transfer of some resources from activities that are not critical and have some slack to critical activities, in order to reduce their duration (Roy, 2005). Using this method we redistribute resources and accomplish reductions in project duration without incurring any (or significant) additional costs. However the time saved will normally be relatively small compared to the whole project, limiting the method's usefulness.

Work Study techniques

Work Study involves the systematic examination of the methods of performing activities so as to improve the effective use of resources (Kanawaty, 1992). According to Slack et al (2007) it is a generic term for those techniques which are used in the examination of work in order to effect improvements. One such technique is Method study; the systematic recording and critical examination of ways of doing things in order to make improvements (Kanawaty, 1992). Method study, in essence, is looking critically at processes in order to improve performance (Brown et al, 2001).

Roy (2007) proposes that work study techniques should be

employed to every critical activity to seek the possibilities of reducing their duration. Equally these methods can also provide opportunities for cost reduction. However the use of such techniques may be restricted by the limited time available for examining and changing the way in which activities are to be performed.

Crashing networks

Crashing networks is defined as 'the process of reducing time spans on critical path activities so that the project is completed in less time' (Slack et al, 2007, p525). The amount of time by which we can shorten an activity depends on the activity; we may not be able to shorten some activities at all. Likewise, the cost of shortening the duration of an activity depends on the nature of the activity (Heizer & Render, 2004).

The aim is to speed up the project at the least additional cost. Therefore we will need to establish by how much each activity can be shortened, at what cost, and if by doing so the project will in fact finish by the due date.

Normally reducing the time for completion of activities incurs extra cost. This can be as a result of overtime working or the use of additional workforce, use of additional resources such as machinery, or sub-contracting some activities. However, shortening the project duration may not only involve additional costs but also savings; indirect costs such as facilities and equipment, and even labour costs can be saved. In estimating costs, we must also consider the cost savings that may occur. Increasing the direct expenses to speed up a project may produce savings in indirect project costs; If there are any incentives for early completion, or penalties for late completion, these must also be taken into account. The goal is to identify those activities that will reduce the sum of the indirect and direct project costs (Stevenson, 2002).

A simple approach to crashing projects involves four steps (Heizer & Render, 2004):

1. Compute the crash cost per unit of time for each activity.
2. Identify the critical path from the network diagram (and consequently the current project duration).
3. Select the activity from the critical path that has the lowest crash cost per unit of time and reduce it by one unit of time.
4. Update activity times. Go back to step two and repeat the process until the desired project duration has been reached.

The activities that will need to be crashed (i.e. shortened) are those that are on the critical path of our network diagram, since shortening noncritical activities would not have an impact on the total project duration. Of course, for each activity that we shorten, we need to reestablish the critical path so as to ensure that we are shortening critical activities (Stevenson, 2002).

However, in applying the Crashing method, we must keep in mind that the quality of a completed project may be affected by project crashing. Project success does not only involve delivering on time and within the budgeted cost. Success also depends on providing what was expected; if the project's outcome does not perform or performs below the set standard, then the project has failed.

Critical Chain Project Planning

The Critical Chain Project Planning is a planning concept that aims to take advantage of any slack in the existing planning schedule. The theory assumes that activity durations are estimates which include some slack for normal delays. With predefined starting times any time saved from activities that finish early is wasted. Thus, in order to take full advantage of all time saved activities should be started as soon as the preceding activities have finished (Brown et al, 2001). However, the applicability of this theory depends on the nature of the work.

CONCLUSION

As we have seen, project management is a complicated process that requires a variety of different management skills. The project manager needs to identify the work necessary to execute the project, plan the work so that it can be achieved within the set parameters of time cost and scope, monitor & control work progress, activity completion times, costs, resource usage, and performance, while taking into consideration stakeholder views and the project environment.

It is essential that all involved, team members and various stakeholders, gain a clear understanding of the project definition and in particular the scope and the limits of the work that is to be done. Moreover we have referred to the usefulness of various project management tools for planning and control, so as to ensure as far as possible that the project will be completed in time, within budget and to the set specifications.

Managing a project effectively means delivering the desired results on time and within the budgeted cost. Projects often fail due to changes in the project scope or conflicting stakeholder interests; the reason for these failures is consistently found to be inadequate involvement and understanding of the project by stakeholders. We have discussed measures that can be taken to prevent and deal with such eventualities, such as the involvement of all relevant stakeholders in the project definition, the use of a 'statement of work' to communicate the project's objectives and scope, the support of the project champion, and the use of scope change control procedures to filter and limit change requests.

We have established how planning is not a one-off process and how it may be repeated in response to changes in circumstances. Moreover we have referred to the usefulness of standard tools for project management such as network diagrams and critical path analysis to determine the duration of projects and which activities need to be shortened if the project is to be completed sooner.

We looked at the time - cost - scope trade off and how the relationship between these constraints limits our options. Subsequently we have examined methods that can be utilised to get the project back on track, such as the Tradeoff of resources, through the use of Work Study techniques, Project Crashing, and Critical Chain Project Planning.

As we have seen Work Study techniques and the Trade-off method may shorten the duration of critical activities without incurring additional costs or even producing cost savings. If this is not sufficient, then the Project Crashing method can be employed, though this method involves extra cost because of the use of additional workforce, equipment, or other inputs. Lastly, Critical Chain Project Planning can be used in planning the updated schedule in order to take advantage of any slack in the time estimates of activities.

REFERENCES

1. Bamford D. & Forrester P., 2010. Essential Guide to Operations Management: Concepts and Case notes. Chichester: John Wisley & Sons

2. Brennan L., 2011. Operations Management. New York: McGraw-Hill

3. Brown S, Blackmon K, Cousins P & Maylor H., 2001. Operations Management: Policy, Practice and Performance Improvement. Oxford: Butterworth-Heinemann

4. Kamauff J., 2010. Manager's guide to Operations Management. New York: McGraw-Hill

5. Lewis, 2007. Fundamentals of Project Management, 3rd Edition. New York: McGraw-Hill

6. PMBOK (A Guide to the Project Management Body of Knowledge), 2004. Pennsylvania: Project Management Institute

7. Rowbotham F., Galloway L. & Azhashemi M., 2007. Operations Management in Context, 2nd edition. Oxford: Butterworth-Heinemann

8. Roy R., 2005. A Modern Approach to Operations Management. New Delhi: New Age International

9. Slack N, Chambers S & Johnston R., 2007. Operations Management, 5th edition. Harlow: Pearson Education

10. Stevenson W., 2002. Operations Management, 7th edition. New York: McGraw-Hill

11. Babu & Suresh, 1996. Project management with time, cost, and quality considerations. Journal of Operational Research. 88, p. 320-327

12. Brennan L., 2011. Operations Management. New York: McGraw-Hill

13. Brown S, Blackmon K, Cousins P & Maylor H., 2001. Operations Management: Policy, Practice and Performance Improvement. Oxford: Butterworth-Heinemann

14. Heizer J. & Render B., 2004. Operations Management, 7th edition. Upper Saddler River, New Jersey: Prentice-Hall

15. Kanawaty G., 1992. Introduction to work study, 4th edition. Geneva, International Labour Office

16. Khang D. and Myint Y., 1999. Time, cost and quality trade-off in project management: a case study. International Journal of Project Management. 17 (4), pp. 249-256

17. Lewis, 2007. Fundamentals of Project Management, 3rd Edition. New York: McGraw-Hill

18. Rowbotham F., Galloway L. & Azhashemi M., 2007. Operations Management in Context, 2nd edition. Oxford: Butterworth-Heinemann

19. Roy R., 2005. A Modern Approach to Operations Management. New Delhi: New Age International

20. Slack N, Chambers S & Johnston R., 2007. Operations Management, 5th edition. Harlow: Pearson Education

21. Stevenson W., 2002.   Operations Management, 7th edition. New York: McGraw-Hill

I hope you have enjoyed PROJECT MANAGEMENT: Introduction to Project Management for Business Students.

For any suggestions or comments please email us at info@mccebooks.com

Webpage: https://www.mccebooks.com

Follow us on Pinterest (Pinner - Mccebooks) and Twitter (@MCCebooks) for continuous new material (articles, study material, etc) for your studies.

Visit our Facebook page (MCCebooks), Like and Follow for updates and to receive special offers and FREE material!

Visit my Amazon Author page for further details on all my Books & eBooks
http://www.amazon.com/Mario-Chinas/e/B00PCN1WFC/

INDEX

Index pages are accurate for 6" by 8" inch page and Arial font size 11

OTHER BOOKS BY THE AUTHOR

EFFICIENT MARKET HYPOTHESIS: Introduction to the Efficient Market Hypothesis for Business Students

VISION AND MISSION: Introduction to Vision and Mission for Business Students

PERCEPTION: Introduction to Perception for Business Students

QUESTIONNAIRES: Short Guide to Questionnaire Design for Business Students

GROUPS IN ORGANISATIONS: Introduction to Work Groups for Business Students

MARKETING RESEARCH: Introduction to Marketing Research for Business Students; Including case study - Coca Cola: The New Coke Debacle

Visit our webpage for the full range of Books and purchase options.

Webpage: https://www.mccebooks.com

PROJECT MANAGEMENT

Introduction to Project Management for Business Students

ISBN: 978-9925-7383-4-2

SECOND EDITION

www.ingramcontent.com/pod-product-compliance
Lightning Source LLC
Chambersburg PA
CBHW022058190326
41520CB00008B/801